365 Days of Positivity

Laura J. Peck

365 Days of Positivity Copyright © 2013 by Laura J. Peck
All rights reserved.
ISBN: 1481906666
ISBN-13:978-1481906661

First Edition

For my sister, Mary F. Bock
Thank you for always believing
Thank you for always staying positive
Thank you for watching over all of us
You are missed, you will be loved forever
This book is for you and for all that believe
in the true spirit of being positive

Always act as if it were impossible to fail!
 -Dr. Norman Vincent Peale (1898-1993)

CONTENTS

Introduction

- January-Start of the New Year, New You
- February-Love of the Month
- March-Lucky You
- April-It's My Birthday
- May-Showers to Flowers
- June-No Gloom in Here
- July-Be Independent
- August-Summer Time Happiness
- September-Work to Live Free
- October-Life is Not Scary
- November-Give Thanks Everyday
- December-Be Born Again

*Note: This book was made for you to discover you by words, not by pages hence no page numbers. Write, mark, fold pages over, do whatever you want to do as to remind you of what quotes/words are important to you. Enjoy the freedom:)

INTRODUCTION

This book has been in the works for I really don't know how long. It seems like forever, but I believe more in the past five years. It was not until this past summer that I began to really want to write a book that was simple, but capable of getting others to see how wonderful they are.

I had come home to assist my parents out after my Dad had been in the hospital. The decision to come home was not an easy one, but a quick one. I struggled with what I could do, but out of the blue it hit me one day to step into the unknown and see what would happen. I had been living in Los Angeles for the past seven years and was really working on trying to find my way. I had gotten to a point in my life that stress and worry was not worth it anymore. It never got me anywhere so why keep putting up with it. I was beginning to learn more about me, what made my life worth moving forward and understanding how being positive can have a wonderful affect on someone.

Before I decided to come home I really put in effort in starting to learn more about being positive and letting go. I was reading books by Dr. Wayne W. Dyer, Gary Zukav, Rhonda Byrne and any other author I could find that discussed how to change one's mentality. I will admit at first that I was not sure it was possible with the negative mentality I held onto for so long. It was not easy, but no matter the setbacks, the mental walls I ran into, I kept telling myself to keep moving and don't stop. The key I found out and still discover everyday as I work on myself to be a more positive person is that I have to keep moving forward. There will be walls, there will be others who try to push you back, but you will get to a point that those things don't have an affect on you anymore. You will see that there is always an opportunity to learn and a positive side to anything negative thrown your way.

This book is a start for me to assist others in changing their mentality and becoming a positive person. This book is your opportunity to take each day and discover the positive it has to offer you. Each day your are given a positive quote (positive word in bold) that I believe you deserve to listen to with all your heart, soul and mind. You are worth more than you could ever have imagined. The possibilities to become the person you were meant to be start with you.

Use this book till it tears apart and you have to get a new one.
Share this book with others and let us change the world around us.

To you and to Positivity Rules!

January

Start of the New Year, New You

With the beginning of the new year, we all make that yearly resolution(s) to become a better person overall. Why? Why don't we make it an everyday resolution? The truth is that it should be a daily process that we should work on over our lifetime. Wake up everyday to working on a new you and see what magic appears in your life. To your journey, we start with the resolute **January**.......

January 1st

Start you life out every New Year with **adventure**.
What an awesome way to learn what you are made of,
who you areand what difference you can make in this world.

January 2nd

Remember that you are **capable** of anything and being anybody.

January 3rd

You are **energetic** in everything you do. The positive energy that surrounds you will always move you forward.

January 4th

There is no need for explanation......you are **fabulous** in every way possible.

January 5th

Last year is over and you cannot change the past so be **healed** from it and start a a new path to being positive everyday.

January 6th

Be **inspired** to do something unbelievable.

January 7th

Life is **magical** so why don't you live it that way.

January 8th

Be **secure** in who you are, where you are going and what you want to do.

January 9th

You are **unique** in your own way. Why be like everyone else?

January 10th

Your **value** on this Earth is more than you will ever know.

January 11th

Being **youthfu**l at any age is about living life to the fullest.

January 12th

Always do your **best** because your **best** is good enough.

January 13th

Discover everyday how important it is for you to be here in this world not only for yourself, but for those that love you.

January 14th

Look in the mirror and tell yourself how **gorgeous** you are.

January 15th

Be **kind** to all those around you and see the rewards that you will receive.

January 16th

Live a life that matters everyday.

January 17th

With the New Year just beginning, always be **optimistic** that the goals you set for yourself will be accomplished because you deserve the best out of life.

January 18th

Life is **plentiful** in what it gives you.

January 19th

Life is **radiant** with you in it.

January 20th

Be **truthful** to yourself.

January 21st

You are **worthy** of everything that you get and earn.

January 22nd

Always have a **zest** for life.

January 23rd

Stay **active** in your physical, your mental, your emotional and your spiritual self. This will be a way to live longer, live vibrant and live prosperous.

January 24th

You will always be **blessed** no matter what.

January 25th

Be **confident** in who you are, what you want, where you want to go and success will always come knocking at your door.

January 26th

Exude your **dazzling** personality everyday.

January 27th

Life is **effortless** if you just let it be.

January 28th

Be **fortunate** in everything that you have around you everyday.

January 29th

One of the simplest things to tell yourself everyday is that life is **good**.

January 30th

Make it a goal everyday to be **healthy**.

January 31st

Be **irresistible** to that special someone.

February

Love of the Month

Oh February how I love thee. The one month with the one day where we celebrate love which I don't truly understand, but I will not knock it down. Sometimes we do need reminders, but I believe and will always believe that love should be celebrated every day for the rest of your life. So, to you **February**, I give all my love to you (and to the rest of the year:)…..

<u>February 1st</u>

Life is **limitless**.

<u>February 2nd</u>

Stay **motivated** to keep moving forward.

<u>February 3rd</u>

Be **noble** in all your efforts.

<u>February 4th</u>

You are an **outstanding** person made for this world we live in.

<u>February 5th</u>

You are **perfect** in every way.

<u>February 6th</u>

Take time to **relax** in each moment that surrounds you.

February 7th

You are a **strong** and independent individual.

February 8th

You are a **talented** individual that thrives on any challenge given to you.

February 9th

You are **victorious** in how you live your life.

February 10th

Be that **wonderful** person that those closest to you know is **wonderful**.

February 11th

Feel **young** from morning till night.

February 12th

You should feel **amazing** everyday you wake up.

February 13th

Always have a **beaming** smile when around others and even when looking into a mirror.

February 14th

Love unconditionally yourself, **love** unconditionally your family,
love unconditionally your closest friends
and **love** unconditionally the **love** of your life.
Love infinitely.

February 15th

Be **clear** and truthful in all your intentions.

February 16th

Life is **delicious** especially if chocolate is involved.

February 17th

Live an **exceptional** life because you are an **exceptional** person.

February 18th

You are **free** to be whomever you want to be.

February 19th

Look in the mirror everyday and tell yourself,
"I am a **great** person."

February 20th

Always be **helpful** to those who might need it.

February 21st

You do have **innovative** ideas that will not only change the world, but change you.

February 22nd

Knowing the real you is what matters the most.

February 23rd

You are **masterful** in your abilities and talent.

February 24th

Neat is just a cool word in itself so use it often.

February 25th

Life is **precious** in every moment so don't waste it on negativity because negativity does not count anymore in your life.

February 26th

You are a **reliable** person that those that matter the most can come to no matter the situation.

February 27th

Be **sensitive** to others who have not yet reached the beautiful space that you are in.

February 28th

You are **thriving** in all that the Universe has given you.

March

Lucky You

Welcome to March and the luck of life. You should always remember that you are here for a reason and we are lucky to have you. You should also remember that you are lucky to have us. As human beings we are here to assist each other in achieving our dreams. Of course there might always be the luck of the Irish in our hands, but the reality is that we make our own luck by being here, by having a positive attitude, by living our dreams and never giving up no matter what. But, still it doesn't hurt to have that lucky charm in hand. To you **March**, I hand over my four leaf clover....

March 1st

Life is so **versatile** that you can do anything you want to.

March 2nd

Be **wise** in your decisions.

March 3rd

Appreciate every thing that surrounds you.
Appreciate those who truly care and love you.
But, most of all **appreciate** who you are
and who you are becoming.

March 4th

You have a **bright** future ahead of you.

March 5th

Be and stay **connected** to the Universe.

March 6th

You are a **dynamic** person
who deserves the best of all worlds.

March 7th

You are **exquisite** in your inner beauty.

March 8th

Everyday you get up and move forward,
your are **fulfilling** all
dreams you have set for yourself.

March 9th

You have an **enormous** gift and talent that needs
to be shown to the world.
Don't hide from it, but find it and release it to the world.

March 10th

Be **generous** with the time that is given to you.

March 11th

When everything you do falls into a place
of peace and kindness, your life becomes
more **harmonious** and more amazing.

March 12th

The **ideal** life you have always wanted is in your hands.
All you have to do is go after it.

March 13th

You have this **keen** understanding of who you are and
no one can take that away from you.

March 14th

You have this unbelievable, **luminous** light about you that
will never be extinguished.

March 15th

You are **mighty** powerful when you want to be to get through,
to get over and to get pass those who try to stop you
in your tracks to success. Use that positive power
to conquer all that stands in your way.

March 16th

Nurture yourself to a place of peace and kindness.

March 17th

You have the **luck** of all that is good and kind in this world.

March 18th

Be an **original** you.

March 19th

Have a **profound** affect on those around you and this world.
It will be an act you will never, ever forget.

March 20th

You are a **quintessential** part of this universe that will have
an everlasting impact.

March 21st

Reward yourself and others for good deeds, for stepping out of
your comfort zone and for making a difference.

March 22nd

You are **stunning** in your beauty, your smile
and everything that you do.

March 23rd

All that is against you will be **triumphed** by you.

March 24th

Make a **valiant** effort everyday to be you, to make a difference,
to love, to be kind, to be human and all that will bring peace
and humanity to this universe.

March 25th

One day know that the **whole** world will come together in peace because you chose to become **whole** as a person.

March 26th

Life is **yummy** especially when it includes chocolate:)

March 27th

Get **zany** every once in awhile because it will remind you of how much fun life really is.

March 28th

Be **authentic** and real because those who know you will appreciate it.

March 29th

You are **blessed** each and everyday.

March 30th

Be **courageous** and step outside your comfort zone. Courage will lead you to a life you have always imagined.

March 31st

Believe in **divine** intervention.

April

It's My Birthday

Oh yes this month is my birthday and I am sure quite a few of you who have graciously bought my book have a birthday this month as well. To you I extend my congratulations for buying this book and wanting to change your life, but I also wish you the Happiest of Birthdays. This is not to say everyone else's birthday is not important. We are all important because we were born. **April** you may bring showers, but we celebrate you always by blowing out those awesome candles.....

April 1st

Life is **easy** if you just let it be.

April 2nd

Life provides many **fascinating** scenes,
many **fascinating** opportunities and many **fascinating** people
so step outside to find them and enjoy them.

April 3rd

Be a **genuine** human being.

April 4th

Everyone has a little **humor** in them including you
so why don't you share that with others.

April 5th

You have **intuitive** abilities to know what is right for you.

April 6th

Jump for joy every chance you get.

April 7th

Be **mindful** of others feelings.
They might not be where you are at
which gives you the opportunity to show them
the way to a more positive and fulfilling life.

April 8th

Everyday is a **new** day.

April 9th

You are an **outgoing** person who truly enjoys
all that life has to offer.

April 10th

You are such a positive person that you are able to **persevere**
through anything that comes your way.

April 11th

Being here is an opportunity to do **remarkable** things
because you are a **remarkable** person.

April 12th

You are a **superb** human being.

April 13th

Every day you step outside your door is a **thrilling** adventure that is not to be missed.

April 14th

Find that **vivid** imagination of yours to accomplish your goals and to bring you new opportunities to be successful at life.

April 15th

Being **wealthy** means having all the love in world that you deserve.

April 16th

You are **accomplished** in your life.

April 17th

Be **bold** in your goals in life.

April 18th

Find **calmness** in a world where fast pace is normal.

April 19th

Life is **daring** in itself so why follow the norm when you have a **daring** life you can follow.

April 20th

Eloquence is found in the written word. Read to find it.

April 21st

A true **friend** is one that supports
and loves you no matter what.

April 22nd

You are rich in all the **glowing** colors
of nature that surround you.

April 23rd

Always work on being an **honest** human being.

April 24th

Be **invincible** in mind, body and spirit.

April 25th

Life is full of **miracles**...
you just have to believe in it every single day.

April 26th

Being **nice** is being you.

April 27th

Be **proud** of all you have done and all that you are.

April 28th

A **radiant** sunshine follows you everywhere you go.

April 29th

Remember no matter where you are, you are **safe** in someone's mind, heart and soul.

April 30th

Always live a **terrific** life.

May

Showers to Flowers

As spring arrives and the flowers start the bloom, life seems to open up because those cold winter nights and all the snow are leaving for better days. Well, ok some of us don't have to worry about the cold or the snow, but we still appreciate the essence of spring and the lovely smell of flowers. So, here is to the beginning of tanning season and the true warmth of the sun....thank you **May** for existing.....

May 1st

Life is as **adorable** as a puppy.

May 2nd

Always stay **centered** with the Universe/Higher Power.

May 3rd

Brilliance lies within you so go out and discover it.

May 4th

Be **determined** in what you do, in who you are
and where you belong.

May 5th

Life is **endless** in its opportunities to be free,
to be courageous and to take pride in who you are
and where you come from.

May 6th

All is **fair** in life and love.

May 7th

You are **gifted** in many ways so why not find these gifts and share them with others.

May 8th

Find **harmony** in the music of life.

May 9th

You being here in this beautiful universe is **impressive**.

May 10th

You are **mighty** in strength, love and happiness.

May 11th-Natural

It is **natural** to have moments, but in those moments look to nature to bring you back to the here and now.

May 12th

The most **powerful** person you will ever know in your lifetime is your Mother. She would do anything to protect you and keep you safe. Thank her, love her and become like her.

May 13th

Work everyday to become a **refined** human being willing to do whatever it takes to make this a more **refined** world.

May 14th

Share all that you are and all that you have
because it is the right thing to do.

May 15th

Trust is something earned and should never be taken for granted.

May 16th

Be **well** with your wishes to all others.

May 17th

Whatever cause you are involved, find your **zeal** to make it
just as important to others as it is to you.

May 18th

Always know that you are **admired** for who you are,
what you do and what you stand for.

May 19th

The only person that can **complete** you is you.

May 20th

Life is **delicious** with all the many different kinds of foods
it has to offer to feed your soul.

May 21st

Be **eager** to go outside the box, to learn something new everyday and to not be afraid to expand on who you are.

May 22nd

Take the time to **flourish** in all that surrounds you.

May 23rd

Always make a **grand** entrance into life.

May 24th

Happiness is you.

May 25th

You have all the **imagination** to be whatever you want.

May 26th

Kudos to you and all that you do everyday.

May 27th

Memories remind us of all that is good in this world and all those who did good that let us be free.

May 28th

Be **productive** in everything you do because those little things add up to big things.

May 29th

Take little moments to **refresh** yourself so that you are ready for anything that comes your way.

May 30th

You are **smart** so do something about it.

May 31st

Live the **ultimate** life.

June

No Gloom in Here

There is this phenomenon in Los Angeles that happens every June. It seems that the ocean fog comes in and takes over the city during this month. I have experienced it for the last seven years and luckily I live further in so it clears up a lot quicker than if you lived at the beach. Now, I love my sunshine and the benefits it has and I know that the sun is not always around during the year, but that should never be an excuse not to enjoy life. This is the time to understand that though the sun might not shine everyday outside, that it should always be shining inside of you. **June** in LA you might cause a gloom on the outside, but we all know that the real, true sunshine always lives inside of us......

<u>June 1st</u>

Take **pride** in who you are.

<u>June 2nd</u>

Wake up every morning with a **vibrant** life that is unstoppable.

<u>June 3rd</u>

The stars are always **aligned** for you.

<u>June 4th</u>

Show off that **cheerful** smile of yours every single day.

<u>June 5th</u>

A **delightful** way to be you is to to be you.

June 6th

Elegance is not the way you dress, but in the way you walk with confidence, strength, love, character, personality, happiness and life.

June 7th

Remember how **fun** it was to play when you were a child with no care in the world? Well, what is stopping you from having **fun** like that now.....nothing I say.

June 8th

Take a walk and see how **interesting** life is.

June 9th

You are **m-a-r-v-e-l-l-o-u-s**.

June 10th

Notice all others around you that could use a little hand to lift their spirits.

June 11th

You are **passionate** about making the world a better place.

June 12th

Give **respect**, get **respect**.

June 13th

You are **successful** in your life
because you get up every new morning.

June 14th

Like **totally**...your awesome:)

June 15th

You have a **voice** so let it be heard in a positive manner.

June 16th

Always remember the **warmth** of your Father's hugs
because it is something that cannot be replaced.

June 17th

Sometimes you just need to scream **Yay!** out loud
to let everyone know how happy you are
and how great life is.

June 18th

Be **alive**.

June 19th

You can **begin** again no matter the circumstances.

June 20th

There is a certain **charm** about you that everyone notices.

June 21st

Life is like a **dance** so why not get down and boogie with it.

June 22nd

Experience everything you can.

June 23rd

Be **fearless** in your efforts to change yourself to be that person you want to be.

June 24th

The universe is **glad** that you are here.

June 25th

Be someone's **hero**.

June 26th

You are an **intelligent** human being.

June 27th

Laugh as often as you can with life and at life.
If you can **laugh** with life and at life
than you are truly living.

June 28th

You are **magnificent** in all that you do for yourself,
for others and for Mother Earth.

June 29th

Peaceful is your heart, mind and soul.

June 30th

Add a little **sparkle** to your day.

July

Be Independent

Fireworks, magic and independence are celebrated this lovely and sometimes sweltering month of July. I believe that we should celebrate our independence every day for so many fought for our rights to be independent. We should live day by day relishing in that fact and truly enjoy it each and every minute of the day. So many others don't have this opportunity so why not celebrate your independence and celebrate that one day others will get their chance. For **July**, we salute you, we send out big flashes of light and hope that independence will always be here to stay.....

July 1st

You have all the power to **tell** everyone that you love and care about how important they are to you.

July 2nd

There is a **vision** that is meant for you...
you just have to go out and see it.

July 3rd

Be **awake** to the life that is handed to you everyday.

July 4th

Be bold, be **big** in celebrating this day of Independence because others fought hard for you to have it.

July 5th

All that is **certain** is that you are here on this Earth for a reason....
a reason only known to you to find,
to discover and to bring to life.

July 6th

Devote your life to helping others succeed and see the many rewards that come your way.

July 7th

Engage yourself in interesting and challenging conversations everyday. See how it lets you grow into a true and wonderful human being.

July 8th

Everyday is a **fine** day to live life.

July 9th

Plant seeds of **gratitude** everyday.

July 10th

Give a free **hug** today and tomorrow and the next day and so on.

July 11th

Invite love into your home.

July 12th

It is a **jolly** day to celebrate whatever you want to celebrate.

July 13th

You are as **likable** as a chocolate fudge sundae.

July 14th

Nothing is more **nifty** than getting excited about your success.

July 15th

Be **prepared** for great things coming your way.

July 16th

Be **reasonable** in your judgments of others
until you hear the real truth from them.

July 17th

It is such a **splendid** day to go outside
and play just as you did when you were a child.
Being adult does not mean you can't have anymore
of those **splendid** and wonderful days.

July 18th

You are **tenacious** in your efforts to succeed at life.

July 19th

Go on, you can say **Yabba Dabba Doo** just like Fred Flinstone
because you can and it would be fun to do it:)

July 20th

There are many **attractive** qualities about you
that are not only on the outside, but on the inside too.

July 21st

There is a **benefit** of having you here today,
tomorrow and from now on.

July 22nd

Make a **conscious** effort to seek growth, to seek understanding,
to seek peace, to seek love from all that is around you.

July 23rd

Excellence is in you.

July 24th

Give a **flattering** compliment to a stranger today.
See them change in that instant to a better person
because you did.

July 25th

Get **giddy** over the one you truly love everyday
because what you have with them is priceless.

July 26th

Being **humble** in what you have is being real and true.

July 27th

Invent a new way of being.

July 28th

Be **merry** in your own little way.

July 29th

Your **persistence** to get through many challenges will open many doors to success.

July 30th

You were built to be **robust** because there is no challenge you cannot get through.

July 31st

You will never be **satisfied** until the world is a better place for all to live a great life.

August

Summertime Happiness

Though summer has officially been upon us for a couple of months already, it is the month of August that tends to stand out more. Probably because everyone is trying to enjoy that last of it before heading back to school and parents getting back into full swing of that constant on the go feeling. I say rather than be unhappy because your freedom is ending, be happy because you are heading into something new and exciting. Making new friends, meeting new goals, enjoying so much more of what summer means, seeing new things, but most of all growing up. As adults, responsibility tends to takeover, but we forget that especially when we have kids. We should adore the time and the serenity of calmness that summer brings. **August** you might be the end of one beautiful season, but you really are the beginning of anew to more than you will ever know....

August 1st

Transcend above all that is not right in this world and work to make it better.

August 2nd

Once you **understand** who you are, you can begin to **understand** how you can help others achieve greatness.

August 3rd

The only person you need to **validate** is yourself.

August 4th

Win at life.

August 5th

Xerox your life into an original.

August 6th

Say **yes** to you.

August 7th

Find your **zenith** and never let go of it.

August 8th

Agree to be human in heart, soul and spirit.

August 9th

Find you state of **bliss** and let it be.

August 10th

Clever is your heart in knowing what it wants.

August 11th

Donate your time and volunteer.

August 12th

Look to the sky and see how **enticing** nature is.
It knows how to enjoy life so why
don't you follow in its footsteps.

August 13th

Your success is **fruitful**.

August 14th

Be **gentle** and kind.

August 15th

Hope is all around you.

August 16th

Take time to **innovate** ways that allow you to move forward in life.

August 17th

Keep your light inside always shining for others to see you as you truly are.

August 18th

Motivate others to be better versions of themselves.

August 19th

Always **nourish** your soul with love.

August 20th

Go outside and **play** as if you were 5 years old again.

August 21st

You are the only one to be **qualified** as you.

August 22nd

Reach for the sky....**reach** for the stars....**reach** for the sun....**reach** for the universe....**reach** for infinity.

August 23rd

The feeling of being **serene** runs through the core of your soul.

August 24th

Teach the next generation the importance of kindness, love and being human.

August 25th

You are **unlimited** in your potential.

August 26th

Make a **wish** upon any star, believe in that wish and see it come true.

August 27th

What an **astounding** life you have.

August 28th

Believe in a destiny....**believe** that you have a destiny.... **believe** in your destiny.

August 29th

Create a life that you will never, ever forget.

August 30th

You are one **dandy**, one of a kind human being.

August 31st

Hold those close to you letting them know how important they are to you.

September

Work to Live Free

Fall into September and learn that life is not about living to work, but working to live. There is this so called holiday in September that is called Labor Day. Labor Day celebrates the worker and I can tell you that a lot of workers love this day. But, the reality is that we work so hard that we forget how to live. We go and go and go to get somewhere not realizing that sometimes we don't go anywhere. Life is about living. Life is about enjoying those around us. Life is about enjoying nature and the peace it offers us. I always fought with the working world because I always felt like I was missing out on something. Now that I am working for myself, I now I understand what I was missing. No more I say for **September** I am working to live life today and everyday....

September 1st

Enhance your vision to always be a person that everyone can look up to.

September 2nd

Any day that gives you time to be with your family and friends is a **festive** day.

September 3rd

Be **gracious** in what is given to you by the universe.

September 4th

Take the time to **improve** yourself everyday.

September 5th

You are a **kindhearted** person that looks for the good and best out of everyone.

September 6th

When the sun rises it is **majestic**.
When the sun sets it is **majestic**.
When the world sees the good in you,
you are just as **majestic** as sunrises and sunsets.

September 7th

Now is your time. Always remember that.

September 8th

A **positive** person lives a **positive** life.

September 9th

Be **real** to yourself, to your family, to your friends
and to the world.

September 10th

Be **sensible** in your decisions and
how they may affect others.

September 11th

United we will be.

September 12th

Be part of a **team** that makes a difference.

September 13th

Wonder is found all around you.

September 14th

Yearn for something better.

September 15th

Achieve beyond what you are capable of.

September 16th

Bright is the light in you.

September 17th

Be **considerate** of others.

September 18th

Be **diligent** in all that you do to be successful.

September 19th

Show **enthusiasm** not only when you succeed,
but when you fail because it shows you that
you are one step closer to succeeding
in something bigger than you could have ever imagined.

September 20th

Every step forward you take is as **graceful** as a dancer.

September 21st

Handsome are you from the outside in.

September 22nd

It only takes one **idea** to be the greatest one.

September 23rd

Find your best **jovial** mood and
pass it along to those you meet everyday.

September 24th

Manifest your destiny. You are the only one that can do it.

September 25th

Quick are you on your feet to save the day for those in need.

September 26th

Rise to any occasion that is put on your plate.

September 27th

You are **successful** in everything you want to do.

September 28th

It is **true**….someone does love you for you.

September 29th

You have an unbelievable, **vivacious** personality that those who know it, see it.

September 30th

Be a thoughtful and gracious **winner**.
Celebrate it with everyone.

October

Life is Not Scary

The costumes and the scariness start to come out this time of year. I am not fond of scary movies though one of my friends somehow gets me to watch them every once in awhile. Dressing up, scaring others is great fun, but the truth is that life is not as scary as we make it out to be. I used to live in fear on a constant basis because I always saw the worse when in reality I had no idea what the future was going to be about. We have the ability, we can make the choice to live a life full of happiness, love, kindness and no fear. Once you realize that life is awesome, you have nothing to be scared of....really nothing. So, Boo! **October** is about fun and not being afraid to live life having fun every day....

October 1st

Wake up every morning and say
"**Yeah** this day is going to be awesome!"

October 2nd

You have so much **zip** that you are capable of doing anything and everything.

October 3rd

Your heart has an **abundance** of love to give away so give it to those that matter, those that need a little love here and there and to those that need a lot of it.
Remember the more you give, the more you will receive.

October 4th

Just **being** you is enough.

October 5th

Life is all about being **creative**.

October 6th

Believe in some kind of **divine** intervention
and when it happens be thankful for it.

October 7th

You are an **efficient** human being that does
what should be done to change what is around you.

October 8th

Follow the **flavorful** colors of life.

October 9th

Find your **garden** and let it grow into this
magnificent human being called you.

October 10th

Hear the sounds of life, remember how beautiful
they are and truly begin to believe in living.

October 11th

Inspire the young, the old, the different to invest in themselves,
to invest in others and to invest in life.

October 12th

The world hit the **jackpot** when you were born.

October 13th

Find the **kaleidoscope** in the sky and see how wonderful life is when you go along with the changes that are meant for you.

October 14th

You are a **lovable** human being. Don't ever forget that.

October 15th

You are **meant** for something bigger than your self.

October 16th

What a **novel** idea for the universe to bring you here to this wonderful world.

October 17th

You are your own **parade** so celebrate you everyday.

October 18th

Relax and release those things that are not you.

October 19th

Look and listen to find the **spiritual** self that allows you to bring others together to change the world for the better.

October 20th

You have a **transparent** truth that shows your inner beauty.

October 21st

Unconditional love is alive. Watch a child, look at their smile and see it through their eyes.

October 22nd

You have an unbreakable **vitality** that can walk through walls.

October 23rd

Wow! You are an incredible human being that deserves the best out of life.

October 24th

Be **yourself**. That is all that should be ever asked of you.

October 25th

Be part of an **affluent** society that is rich in kindness and love.

October 26th

Your love is **bountiful**.

October 27th

Choose your life and live it in complete harmony with the Universe.

October 28th

Let everyone see that **dashing** and beautiful smile you have.

October 29th

Be **enthusiastic** about life and all the wonderful things about it.

October 30th

Family does matter.

October 31st

Go out, be you and celebrate life.

November

Give Thanks Everyday

Oh you know when November comes around that you are going to have to unbuckle the belt and undo your pants. But, November is not all about turkey and pie, it is also about giving thanks. Truth be told, we should always give thanks everyday we are here….just not on one day where we feast like tomorrow is going to end. One aspect of my life I learned this past year is that I never gave enough thanks or even gratitude for all that I have gotten and all that I have now. Well, this year and every year including **November**, I plan on giving thanks every single day and hope that you start the same as well…….

<u>November 1st</u>

Always give a **hand** to someone that needs it to show them that they are capable of being better than where they are at now.

<u>November 2nd</u>

You have an **impeccable** way about you that sends goodness out into the world.

<u>November 3rd</u>

Believe that **time** is on your side.

<u>November 4th</u>

How can you not be **jubilant** when your life is magnificent.

<u>November 5th</u>

You have this **knack** to change others for the better.

November 6th

Be a **leader** that looks to make changes for all
and for the better.

November 7th

Take the time to **make** a difference.

November 8th

What could be more beautiful than being one with **nature**.

November 9th

Keep turning the **page** of your life and see all
the wonderful stories you will be making.

November 10th

You are a **resourceful** person
when it comes to finding solutions.

November 11th

You are a **sensational** person that does so much for others.

November 12th

Always be **teachable** because what you can learn
from others could change your life.

November 13th

Life is **ultra** awesome.

November 14th

Victory is yours.

November 15th

Woo Hoo! Great things will happen to you today and everyday.

November 16th

You are in the **zone**.

November 17th

Your **artistic** abilities are amazing, soulful, full of change and true love.

November 18th

Bring your light into the world.

November 19th

Life is a **cabaret** that you should be a part of.

November 20th

Always make an **deposit** of goodness into your heart, soul and mind.

November 21st

You live an **enlightened** life.

November 22nd

Funny how life works out when you least expect it.

November 23rd

Giving of yourself to make changes for the better is the way life should be.

November 24th

You should strive to be that **happy-go-lucky** person all the time.

November 25th

Be an **inspiration** to yourself.

November 26th

You are a precious **jewel**.

November 27th

The **key** to your life is inside of you.

November 28th

Be **thankful** for everyday your here.
Be **thankful** for all that you have.
Be **thankful** for all those that surround you.
Be **thankful** on a daily basis.

November 29th

Leap for joy.

November 30th

Your life is a **medley** waiting to be sung.

December

Be Born Again

I would say that December is one of the greatest months out there. I say this because this month we get to buy gifts and hand them out. We also get to receive gifts. How can one not be happy about that? I sure am and what is even better is that it is a chance to get ready to renew ourselves and be born again. This is the last month of the year and while we have fun with giving and receiving , we are also getting prepared for the new year that is heading our way. We get to move on from this year and in some sense start over. But, did you realize that everyday you wake up is a new day? A new day to start over? Why wait till next year when you can start now. Heck why wait till this month to give out all those awesome gifts. Oh **December** with your Santa Claus and reindeer, I love that you let us give so much and celebrate being born again.....

December 1st

All that you will accomplish will be **notable** from now until forever.

December 2nd

Whatever you decide today will **outweigh** all that is behind you. The past is the past.

December 3rd

Always **progress** towards something better.

December 4th

Be **quotable**.

December 5th

Take the time to **rest** your mind, heart and soul as to allow them to grow properly into your truth.

December 6th

Be **self-reliant** as to teach others to be.

December 7th

Taking the time to give is taking the time to be **thoughtful**.

December 8th

You have a spirit that can **uplift** anyone.

December 9th

Take a small **vacation** everyday into your own mind so as to refresh your spirit.

December 10th

Your **well-being** should always be important to you as well as others **well-being**.

December 11th

Yippee! You did it! You are the essence of a true human being.

December 12th

Appear as someone better than you that is out
to make the world a more peaceful and serene place to be.

December 13th

Teach others to **bridge** kindness and love
so that we all can live as one.

December 14th

Be part of a **class** that is rich in humanity.

December 15th

What you seek out of life should be more **desirable**
than any monetary riches because
you are worth more than that.

December 16th

Endow others with the ability to spread kindness
and unconditional love.

December 17th

Feed love into your heart on a daily basis.

December 18th

Your pot of **gold** can be found in your heart.

December 19th

You have been **handpicked** by the universe to
do something so magical that it will change
the world for the better.

December 20th

Make an **imprint** on this world everyday you go out into it.

December 21st

Kiss in the rain and see what magic takes place.

December 22nd

Sing a **lullaby** anytime you can to a child and
see a smile so big that it will warm your heart every time.

December 23rd

There is a **meaning** to your life. You just have to go out
and discover it.

December 24th

You were **born** for a reason and the universe has a plan
for you to succeed in this world.

December 25th

This day should always be a **joyous** occasion to celebrate life.

December 26th

What is **next** for you is a life of worthiness.

December 27th

Open your heart, **open** your soul and the love of your life will walk right in.

December 28th

Paint yourself into a work of art.

December 29th

Rejoice in your life.

December 30th

Sail into a sea of beauty.

December 31st

Today and everyday you can start anew and be better than the day before.

To The New Year

This book was written for you. It was written to push you outside your comfort zone because we all need to go outside and live a life full of adventure. Each day is letting you know that you are perfect, that you are worth it, that you are happy, that you are awesome....that you are love. This is a book that can be used every year for the rest of the life. Whatever you do live your life as if it is magic. Live your life because there is no other way to do it. Nothing is better than living a life of purpose and positivity. Positivity rules and so do you.

To you and Positivity Rules!

Laura J. Peck

Laura J. Peck is a Success Coach that is based out of Los Angeles, California. To learn more about Laura, email her at laurapecksuccesscoach@gmail.com.

Made in the USA
Lexington, KY
13 October 2013